FOREX ZONES

MASTERING SUPPORT AND RESISTANCE, MARKET SENTIMENT, AND PRICE ACTION TO IDENTIFY HIGH-PROBABILITY TRADES

JAMES WILLY

Copyright © 2024 James Willy

All rights reserved.

TABLE OF CONTENT

INTRODUCTION — 7

The Advantages of Trading with Zones — 7

CHAPTER 1 — 15

Understanding the fundamentals of forex trading — 15
- The nature of currency markets. — 15
- How Currency Pairs Work — 16

CHAPTER 2 — 21

The Concept of Trading Zones — 21
- What are Trading Zones — 21
- The Relationship Between Price and Zone — 22
- Why Zones Matter More Than Exact Levels — 23
- Developing Your Trading Zone Mindset — 24

CHAPTER 3 — 27

Mastering Support and Resistance — 27
- The Real Nature of Support and Resistance — 27
- Identifying Strong Support and Resistance Zones — 28
- Dynamic versus Static Zones — 29
- Multiple Timeframe Analysis of Zones — 30

    Zone Strength Assessment   31

    Common Support and Resistance Mistakes   31

CHAPTER 4   35

Market Sentiment Analysis   35

    Understanding Mass Psychology in Forex   35

    Key Indicators of Market Sentiment   36

    Reading Institutional Money Flow   37

    Combining Sentiment and Zone Trading   38

    Contrarian Trading in Zones   38

CHAPTER 5   41

Price Action: The Language of the Market   41

    Core Price Action Patterns   41

    Candlestick Patterns that Matter in Zones   42

    Understanding Price Momentum   43

    Volume Analysis for Forex   44

    Price Action Confirmation Signals   45

CHAPTER 6   49

Combining the Three Pillars   49

    How Support/Resistance, Sentiment, and Price Action Interact   49

    Creating a Zone Trading Framework   50

    Identifying High Probability Setup Criteria   51

    Managing conflicting signals   52

CHAPTER 7 — 55

Entry and Exit Strategies — 55

    Zone-Based Entry Techniques — 55

    Multiple Entry Scenarios — 56

    Exit Strategies for Different Market Conditions — 57

    Partial Position Management — 58

    Scaling in and out of trades — 58

CHAPTER 8 — 61

Risk Management for Zone Trading — 61

    Position Sizing Based On Zones — 61

    Setting Stops with Zone Analysis — 62

    Risk-reward calculations — 63

    Managing Drawdowns — 64

    Portfolio Heat Management — 64

CHAPTER 9 — 67

Advanced Zone Concepts — 67

    Order Flow Analysis — 67

    Market Structure Analysis — 68

    Institutional Trade Zones — 69

    Complex Zone Patterns — 70

    Harmonics and zones — 70

CHAPTER 10 — 73

Building Your Trading Plan ... 73

    Create Your Zone Trading Strategy ... 73

    Test Your Zone System ... 74

    Recordkeeping and Trade Analysis ... 75

    Continuous Improvement Process ... 76

    Psychology & Discipline ... 77

CHAPTER 11 ... 79

Real-World Trading Scenarios ... 79

    Case Study on Major Currency Pairs ... 79

    Case Study: Cross Rates ... 80

    Case Study: Exotic Pairs. ... 81

    Market Condition Analysis ... 82

    Trading Journal ... 83

CHAPTER 12 ... 85

Common Challenges and Solutions ... 85

    Dealing With False Breakouts ... 85

    Managing News Events ... 86

    Handling volatile markets ... 87

    Overcoming Emotional Trading ... 88

    Building Consistency ... 89

CONCLUSION ... 91

Your Journey to Mastery ... 91

Introduction

The Advantages of Trading with Zones

Trading forex is more than just buying and selling currencies; it is also about understanding the invisible zones where market forces intersect. During my fifteen years in the forex market, I've learnt that mastering these zones changes the way you observe price movements, shifting your focus from simple chart patterns to dynamic areas of opportunity.

Allow me to share something personal. During the 2008 financial crisis, I lost roughly 70% of my trading account because I focused on specific support and resistance levels rather than zones.

That horrible experience showed me that the market does not follow precise lines, but rather areas of interest where several traders make decisions.

The FX market swings in sentimental waves, rising and falling like an ocean tide. As traders, we must learn to read these waves inside their own zones, understanding that each currency pair has its own personality and behavioural tendencies. You are not just looking at charts; you are evaluating the combined actions of millions of traders throughout the world.

Trading zones are places where prices have previously exhibited substantial reactivity. Zones provide you more leeway when analysing market behaviour than fixed support and resistance lines. They resemble neighbourhood boundaries rather than exact street addresses. When I began viewing the market through this lens, my trading outcomes improved considerably.

The three foundations of successful zone trading - support and resistance, market sentiment, and price action - interact like pieces in an orchestra. Support and resistance zones form the structure, market sentiment gives momentum, and price action validates the timing. This perfect combination creates high-probability trades.

In the early days of trading, I addressed these elements individually. I'd search for support levels without thinking about sentiment, or track price action without regard for zones. What was the result? Inconsistent performance and disappointing results. One trade that sticks out occurred in EUR/USD: I noticed a beautiful price action setup but disregarded the fact that it was in a weak zone with low sentiment. That trade flopped spectacularly, but it taught me the value of including all three elements.

It is true that the foreign exchange market is open around the clock, but not every hour presents the same opportunities. Certain zones become more important during various trading sessions. For example, during the Asian session, you may see that prices follow distinct zones than during the London open. Understanding these distinctions provides you an advantage when spotting high-probability scenarios.

Here's why zone trading is so powerful: It's consistent with how large institutional traders work. They accumulate and disseminate within zones, rather than entering or exiting positions at specific levels. By understanding this principle, you learn to trade with the smart money rather than against it.

When trading using zones, risk management acquires a new dimension.

Instead of placing stops at precise levels that can be easily picked off, you'll learn how to employ zones to protect your holdings while giving trades room to breathe. This approach has prevented me from being stopped out of potentially successful trades numerous times.

Allow me to tell you about a trade that confirmed my trust in zone trading. In 2015, I was watching USD/JPY consolidate in a zone that had previously served as support. Market sentiment indicators indicated rising bullish pressure, while price action created a definite bottoming pattern. Instead of entering at the first indication of a reversal, I waited for all three elements to align. That patience led to one of my most profitable trades of the year.

This book extends beyond theory. Each chapter relies on actual market experiences, both successes and disappointments.

You will learn not only what and how, but also why each concept exists. The tactics and approaches presented here have been improved over years of market observation and trading.

Through these pages, I'll walk you through the steps of creating your own zone trading system. You'll learn how to find high-probability setups by combining support and resistance zones, market sentiment, and price action. More importantly, you'll grasp how to apply these concepts to your specific trading style and risk tolerance.

Remember that successful trading isn't about forecasting the future; it's about discovering high-probability opportunities and managing risk wisely. Zone trading provides a framework to accomplish both. As you read this book, you'll get a better understanding of market dynamics and the confidence to make trades based on solid analysis rather than emotions or hunches.

The road ahead will test your existing trading views and encourage you to grow as a trader. But I promise you this: if you approach these concepts with an open mind and a desire to understand them, you'll emerge with a powerful set of tools for successfully navigating the forex market.

Let's embark on this adventure together, studying the intriguing world of zone trading and learning how these concepts might improve your trading outcomes.

Chapter 1

Understanding the fundamentals of forex trading

The nature of currency markets.

The foreign currency market is the world's largest financial marketplace, with currencies fluctuating in an ongoing cycle of supply and demand. Unlike traditional markets, forex lacks a central exchange, resulting in a truly global network of banks, institutions, and dealers. Prices can vary greatly across dealers due to their decentralised structure, yet this is precisely what creates profit opportunities.

During my years of trading, I've discovered that the forex market's high daily volume - more than $6 trillion - has distinct advantages. Because of its size, no single institution, including central banks, can sustain price control for an extended period of time. This is especially important when performing trades because it often ensures minimal slippage and quick order fulfilment.

How Currency Pairs Work

Currency trading always involves pairs, which means buying one currency and selling another. When you take a position in EUR/USD, you are expressing your view on the Euro's relative strength against the US Dollar. The base currency (EUR) is mentioned first, followed by the quote currency (USD).

My early trading days taught me that understanding pip values and position sizing is more than just arithmetic; it is critical to survival.

The value of a pip, or smallest price change in forex, varies depending on the size of your position and the currency pair you're trading. For regular lots, each pip in EUR/USD is worth $10, although the value differs between pairs.

Major Trading Sessions and Market Hours

The fact that the forex market is open 24 hours a day does not mean that each hour offers equal opportunity. Through experience, I've identified three major trading sessions: Asian, London, and New York. Each session has an own personality and trading style.

Price movements during the Asian session are often slower and more thoughtful. When London opens, volatility typically increases as European traders enter the market. The main activity frequently occurs during the London-New York overlap, when two major financial centres work simultaneously.

You will notice that certain currency pairs become more active during specific periods. EUR/USD and GBP/USD are the most volatile during London hours, whereas USD/JPY varies dramatically during Asian trading. Understanding these trends allows you to determine the best times to trade your chosen pairs.

The Psychology Behind Successful Trading

Technical analysis and market understanding are just two parts of the trading equation. Numerous traders who had good technical skills failed because they were unable to master their emotions. Fear and greed are regular companions in the market; learning to control them will determine your success.

In my trading experience, I've discovered that maintaining emotional stability is more crucial than finding the correct entry moment.

When your position changes against you, terror can overpower logic. When you're profitable, greed may tempt you to abandon your exit strategy. Both conditions frequently result in losses.

The foundation for consistent results is built by creating a trading strategy and sticking to it regardless of market conditions. Your plan should contain entrance criteria, position sizing, risk management recommendations, and exit strategies. Every good trader I know uses a planned strategy instead than trading intuitively.

The market tests your discipline on a daily basis. One winning trade does not make you a genius, and one loss does not make you a loser. Success comes from staying constant in your approach and learning from both victories and setbacks. I keep track of each trade in my journal, assessing what worked and what didn't, and I'm constantly refining my strategy.

Every market day brings new issues and opportunities. The sooner you accept that some factors are beyond your control, the better your trading decisions will be. Instead than attempting to forecast every market movement, prioritise risk management and strategy execution. This mental shift converts trading from a frenzied guessing game into a structured business activity.

These fundamentals will form the foundation of your forex trading adventure. Master these, and you'll have a good foundation for applying more advanced techniques. The journey ahead requires patience, discipline, and continuous learning, but the rewards make it worthwhile.

Chapter 2

The Concept of Trading Zones

What are Trading Zones?

Trading zones are areas on your charts where the price has shown considerable movement many times. Unlike fixed support and resistance lines, zones cover a larger area where market players make critical buying and selling choices. Through my significant market expertise, I've discovered that zones behave like magnetic fields, attracting and repelling price movements based on their historical relevance.

In the forex market, zones are often several pips wide, producing bands where institutional orders gather.

You'll notice that these areas frequently correspond with round numbers or past important highs and lows. When prices enter these zones, buyer-seller interaction increases, creating possibilities for expert traders.

The Relationship Between Price and Zone

Price interacts with zones in interesting ways. It bounces quickly at times, but it also hovers within the zone before determining where to go next. I've seen that powerful zones frequently force prices to pause down, as if testing the waters before making its next move. This behaviour provides important insights into market mood and prospective trading opportunities.

The strength of a zone grows with each meaningful interaction. When price reaches a zone that has repeatedly demonstrated its significance, market players pay closer attention.

This increased knowledge frequently results in self-fulfilling price fluctuations as traders anticipate specific behaviours inside these areas.

Why Zones Matter More Than Exact Levels.

My pricey market lessons taught me that concentrating on specific levels typically results in frustration and losses. Markets rarely follow accurate prices. Instead, they focus on areas of interest where high numbers of orders accrue. Trading zones recognise this reality and provide a more realistic framework for market analysis.

Consider zones as neighbourhoods rather than specific addresses. Trading zones describe areas where price behaviour changes, just as a neighbourhood has rough bounds rather than specific lines. This broader perspective allows you to avoid the classic pitfall of setting orders at certain levels where pauses frequently gather.

Developing Your Trading Zone Mindset.

Developing a zone trading attitude necessitates moving away from the pursuit for perfect entry positions. Instead, concentrate on understanding how prices behave across different zones. This method is consistent with how institutional traders operate, as they build and disperse positions throughout zones rather than at specific prices.

I've come to see the market as a series of zones where probability favours specific outcomes. This viewpoint alleviates the pressure to capture accurate tops and bottoms. When you've identified a strong zone, your objective is to read price behaviour within it to decide the best trade setting.

The zone attitude also enhances risk management. Rather than setting stops at obvious levels where other traders have clustered their orders, you can make better informed decisions about position sizing and stop placement by considering the entire zone. This method frequently helps to avoid hasty exits while still protecting your cash.

Trading success stems from recognising probability rather than pursuing certainty. Zones let you find areas where the odds shift in your favour. By carefully observing price behaviour within these zones, you will begin to recognise patterns that reoccur across different currency pairs and periods.

Your analysis should consider the interaction of multiple zones. Strong trades frequently arise when many zones match across timeframes. This confluence boosts the likelihood of a successful trades by indicating where various groups of traders concentrate their efforts.

By learning zone analysis, you will have a better grasp of market structure and price behaviour. This knowledge turns your trading from a series of discrete decisions to a cohesive strategy based on market realities.

The ideas presented in this chapter establish the groundwork for combining zone analysis with market emotion and price movement, creating a robust framework for spotting trades with a high probability of success.

Chapter 3

Mastering Support and Resistance.

The Real Nature of Support and Resistance

In forex trading, support and resistance form the foundation of technical analysis. However, most traders misinterpret their genuine nature. Years of market observation have taught me that these are not hard lines, but rather dynamic zones where market psychology shows itself through price movement. When price approaches a support volume zone, buyers enter with sufficient volume to stop the slide. Sellers emerge in resistance zones to cap the advance.

Identifying Strong Support and Resistance Zones.

Strong zones are revealed through repeated price reactions. I seek for areas where price has reversed at least three times, showing that market players understand their importance. The more price reacts to a zone, the more traders pay attention to it, often resulting in self-fulfilling prophecies.

The strongest zones frequently form at critical technical levels, such as prior big highs and lows, round numbers, and high-volume trading areas. Your analysis should centre on how prices respond when they enter these zones. Sharp reversals often signal stronger zones than slow bounces.

Dynamic versus Static Zones

Static zones are fixed on your charts, but dynamic zones move with price. Moving averages provide dynamic zones that shift over time, adapting to changing market conditions. In my trading, I've discovered that combining the two types provides a more comprehensive picture of potential market turning points.

When dynamic zones are combined with static zones, they frequently result in strong arrangements. For example, when a 200-day moving average meets with a static support zone, the combined effect usually results in larger price movements. These confluence locations warrant extra consideration in your analysis.

Multiple Timeframe Analysis of Zones

Each timeline provides a unique story, but when combined, they form a holistic market narrative. Begin using larger timeframes to discover key zones, then descend to smaller timeframes for entry precision. Strong zones on higher timescales frequently impact price behaviour on lower timeframes.

Zones showing relevance over various timeframes have more weight, as I've discovered. When the weekly, daily, and 4-hour charts all show a strong zone, the likelihood of a big price reaction rises dramatically. This alignment of timeframes should be considered while making trading decisions.

Zone Strength Assessment

Not all zones have similar value. The strength of a zone is determined by several parameters, including the frequency of price reactions, the time period, the volume during past interactions, and the sharpness of price reversals. Through practice, you'll gain an instinctive understanding of zone strength.

Price generally performs differently in strong and weak zones. Strong zones usually produce swift, decisive reversals with a lot of volume. Weak zones may see prices float through with no reaction. Understanding these distinctions allows you to optimise your trade entry and exits.

Common Support and Resistance Mistakes.

Many traders make the key mistake of interpreting support and resistance as precise price levels.

This thinking causes tight stops to be activated before the market makes a significant move. Instead, consider these areas to be zones where prices may fluctuate before forming the following trend.

Another common mistake is failing to update zones when market conditions change. Support and resistance are not static concepts; they change with market conditions. Your analysis must be adaptable, adapting to fresh price action that may strengthen or weaken previous zones.

Trading against strong zones is rarely successful. I've seen several traders try to select tops and bottoms while fighting against established zones. Success in forex requires trading with the market's flow rather than against it. When prices reach a strong zone, patience often yields better results than aggression.

The concepts presented here form the basis for successful zone trading. You'll make better trade entry, exit, and risk management decisions by understanding how support and resistance work. The following chapters will expand on this knowledge by showing how to use zone analysis in conjunction with market sentiment and price action to make high-probability bets.

Chapter 4

Market Sentiment Analysis

Understanding Mass Psychology in Forex

Market sentiment has a tremendous impact on currency fluctuations. Fear, greed, confidence, and uncertainty are just a few of the feelings that traders' collectively express through price action. Throughout my trading experience, I've seen how these psychological influences produce predictable results. When the market is in panic, even the best technical setups might fail. During situations of extreme optimism, prices frequently rise above rational levels.

Key Indicators of Market Sentiment

Sentiment manifests itself through a variety of market cues. The Commitment of Traders report reveals the positions of major speculators and commercial traders. I've seen that extreme readings in this data frequently precede major market shifts. When too many traders surge into one side of the market, the risk of a reversal rises.

Interest rate expectations have a big influence on forex sentiment. Central bank policies and economic data releases cause quick shifts in market psychology. Understanding how these fundamental characteristics affect various trader groups is critical. Professional traders frequently position themselves ahead of significant economic events, resulting in visible patterns in price action.

Reading Institutional Money Flow.

Large institutions leave imprints on the market. You will begin to recognise their presence after careful analysis of volume, price action, and order flow. During my trading sessions, I look for signals of institutional activity, such as huge block trades, consistent buying or selling pressure, and unusual options activity.

Bank dealing desks manage huge client order flows, providing them a unique perspective on market dynamics. While you cannot access their order books directly, price action frequently discloses where these orders concentrate. Pay attention to round numbers and past notable highs or lows, as institutional orders tend to cluster around these points.

Combining Sentiment and Zone Trading

Sentiment analysis is very effective when combined with support and resistance zones. Strong zones frequently correspond with extremes in market sentiment. I've seen that when bearish sentiment hits severe levels around solid support zones, big reversals occur.

Your trading selections should be based on sentiment and technical analysis. A support zone becomes more important when combined with oversold conditions and strong bearish positioning. Similarly, resistance zones are more important when overbought conditions and overwhelming bullish sentiment exist.

Contrarian Trading in Zones

Taking contrarian positions at sentiment extremes is frequently the most rewarding trading strategy.

When everyone becomes bearish, smart money tends to accumulate long positions. However, time is key. Even when sentiment indicators indicate probable reversals, I prefer to wait for price action confirmation before trading against the crowd.

Successful contrarian trading needs patience and discipline. The market can sustain intense sentiment for longer than you might expect. Your analysis should include not only sentiment extremes, but also catalysts that may cause sentiment swings. Economic data, central bank moves, and large technical breakouts are common sources of catalysts.

The ability to perceive and analyse market sentiment distinguishes successful traders from the rest. Most traders follow the crowd, buying when others buy and selling when others sell.

You can position yourself ahead of key market moves by understanding sentiment dynamics rather than following them.

Sentiment analysis is useful for identifying probable market turning points, but it should not be used in isolation. For optimal outcomes, combine it with technical analysis and smart risk management. False signals can arise, particularly in trending markets where sentiment extremes may last longer than anticipated.

The principles covered in this chapter provide tools for understanding market psychology and sentiment dynamics. These observations, when combined with support and resistance zones, form an effective framework for discovering high-probability trading opportunities. The following chapter will look at how price action analysis completes the picture by offering specific entry and exit signals for your trades.

Chapter 5

Price Action: The Language of the Market

Core Price Action Patterns

Price action reveals the raw nature of market behaviour. In my years of trading, I've learnt that every price movement has importance. Each candle, swing, and pattern depicts the constant conflict between buyers and sellers. The skill is in appropriately understanding these signals. Strong movements with enormous candles demonstrate conviction, but little bodies with long wicks imply hesitation.

Candlestick Patterns that Matter in Zones

Not all candlestick patterns have equal significance. When trading currencies, some formations are consistently trustworthy. Pin bars forming in strong zones indicate potential reversals. Engulfing patterns depict one side dominating the other. Inside bars represent coiling pressure before to explosive movement.

Trading exclusively on candlestick patterns produces mixed results. The true power emerges when these patterns form within important zones. A pin bar can emerge anywhere on your chart, but when it appears in a major support zone with aligned market sentiment, the chances of a good trades skyrocket.

Understanding Price Momentum

Price momentum indicates the market's underlying strength. Strong trends result in candles moving decisively in one direction. Even when prices reach new highs or lows, weakening momentum is typically seen in the form of shorter candles. I pay great attention to these tiny adjustments since they frequently signal large market shifts.

Your analysis should track momentum shifts over multiple timeframes. The hourly chart can reflect fading momentum while the daily trend remains strong. These divergences open up possibilities for expert traders who understand market dynamics.

Volume Analysis for Forex

Despite the decentralised nature of forex markets, volume analysis gives useful information. Tick volume measures trading activity and indicates when major players enter or depart holdings. High volume in support or resistance zones emphasises their significance. Low volume amid price increases frequently signals unsustainable developments.

I've seen that volume surges frequently precede large market movements. When the price consolidates with diminishing volume, look for a breakout. Sharp volume rises during trends prove their strength, but dropping volume indicates potential weariness.

Price Action Confirmation Signals

Prior to large movements, the market sends forth distinct signals. Double tops and bottoms occur when prices test levels twice before reversing. Trendline breaks indicate changing market dynamics. Flag patterns suggest that the action will continue after a brief pause. These formations allow for more exact timing of entry and exits.

Learning to read price action requires time and practice. Begin by focussing on key patterns in strong zones. A tidy double bottom near support bears more weight than convoluted patterns in randomly selected chart locations. The simplest signals are frequently the most reliable.

You'll develop an intuitive sense for price action over years of screen time. Patterns emerge across various currency pairs and timeframes.

The idea is to recognise these patterns early on and understand how they will affect future price movement.

False signals arise frequently in forex markets. Your success is dependent on integrating price action research with other criteria such as support/resistance zones, market mood, and effective risk management. Although no one indication or pattern is perfect, when used together, they provide a strong trading strategy.

Price action expertise necessitates time and discipline. Avoid pressing trades when clear signals are not available. The best setups frequently occur after periods of quiet trading, when the market provides obvious indications of its upcoming move. Your job is waiting for high-probability scenarios rather than trading every pattern you see.

The concepts discussed here are one component of our entire trading strategy. The following chapter will demonstrate how to combine price action analysis, support/resistance zones, and market sentiment. This integration provides a robust framework for discovering and executing high-probability trades over any timeframe.

Chapter 6

Combining the Three Pillars

How Support/Resistance, Sentiment, and Price Action Interact

When all three factors come together, zone trading reaches its full potential. Support and resistance zones lay the groundwork, market sentiment implies probability, and price action offers exact entry locations. I've learnt over years of trading that these components work together to enhance each other's performance.

Layering these analyses makes trading more precise. When sentiment indicators indicate that the market is oversold, a support zone strengthens. The setup is considerably more appealing when price action produces a reversal pattern within that zone. These confluence moments frequently presage large market movements.

Creating a Zone Trading Framework.

Your trading framework must incorporate all three pillars in a systematic manner. Begin by identifying important support and resistance zones over longer time periods. Then evaluate market sentiment using a variety of indicators and positioning data. Finally, look for certain price action patterns that indicate prospective trades.

I created my framework after years of trial and error. Each trade configuration must meet stringent requirements from all three perspectives. The zones must demonstrate historical relevance. Sentiment should indicate a clear bias. Price action must confirm a possible reversal or continuation.

Identifying High Probability Setup Criteria

High-probability setups have common qualities. Strong zones have multiple historical reactions. Sentiment reaches extremes. Price action follows apparent patterns. The probability of a successful trades increases significantly when these conditions come together.

The most powerful setups frequently emerge amid major market changes. Sentiment reaches bearish extremes near solid support zones. Price forms reversal patterns as volume increases. These situations provide ideal conditions for winning trades. Your objective is to patiently wait for these alignments rather than forcing trades in inferior conditions.

Managing conflicting signals

Markets rarely offer flawless setups. Sometimes sentiment points in one direction while price action points in another. Through experience, I've learnt to prioritise various conflicts based on their importance. Strong zone reactions usually obscure slight sentiment divergences.

When signals contradict, take a step back and reassess. Check several timelines for clarity. When examined from several angles, perceived problems can sometimes resolve themselves. Your analysis should be flexible while keeping to key ideas.

The integration process involves practice and improvement. Each market day provides a different set of indications. Some align flawlessly, while others show perplexing contradictions. Success comes from remaining disciplined while adapting to changing circumstances.

Technical analysis alone is often insufficient. Fundamental factors influence sentiment, which affects how prices react in specific zones. Your framework should consider key economic events and their possible impact on market psychology.

When all three pillars are in alignment, trading decisions become more straightforward. Strong zones with confirming sentiment and unambiguous price action generate the highest probability setups. These scenarios occur infrequently, yet they provide the finest risk-reward potential.

The following chapter investigates various entry and exit options based on this integrated strategy. You'll learn how to place trades when the three pillars align and how to manage holdings when market conditions change. This expertise translates theoretical comprehension into practical trading results.

By consistently applying these concepts, you will get an advantage in the forex market. The combination of support/resistance zones, sentiment analysis, and price action provides a solid framework for selecting and executing profitable trades. Maintain patience, discipline, and trust throughout the integration process.

Chapter 7

Entry and Exit Strategies

Zone-Based Entry Techniques

Entry timing distinguishes profitable trades from losing ones. My technique focusses on specific triggers inside predefined zones. When price reaches a critical zone, I look for confirmation cues, such as powerful candlestick patterns, volume spikes, or momentum shifts. Responding to actual price behaviour is the key, not forecasting reversals.

You'll see that the most profitable entries frequently result from waiting for unambiguous confirmation.

Many traders enter positions too early, expecting to capture the absolute bottom or top. Through experience, I've discovered that giving up a few pips for confirmation produces greater results than attempting to predict exact turning points.

Multiple Entry Scenarios

Different market situations necessitate different entry strategies. During strong trends, trading pullbacks to support or resistance zones is effective. In range markets, entries near zone boundaries produce greater results. Your strategy must evolve to reflect current market circumstances while adhering to basic ideals.

I make entries based on certain price action signals. A pin bar reversal at support may result in an immediate entry.

Other times, breaking into a zone necessitates extra validation. These selections are guided by the zone's strength as well as the wider market context.

Exit Strategies for Different Market Conditions.

Exit strategies are just as important as entries. Profitable trades can turn into losses without suitable exit strategy. Take-profit levels should align with the next important zone. Partial profit-taking at predetermined levels helps protect profits while allowing winners to run.

Your exits must take into account market conditions. Trailing stops keep you in profitable trades for a longer period of time when markets are trending. In volatile markets, tighter exits safeguard profits. After years of trading, I discovered that flexible exit strategies outperform inflexible take-profit levels.

Partial Position Management

Managing positions with partial exits improves overall performance. Taking profits on a portion of your investment at first targets relieves pressure and allows you to make more objective judgements with the remaining lots. This technique combines the advantages of both conservative and aggressive trading strategies.

The first exit frequently occurs at the next resistance zone for longs or support zone for shorts. Additional pieces can target further away zones. This stepwise strategy captures both short-term and long-term trends while efficiently minimising risk.

Scaling in and out of trades

Strategic scaling improves trade management prospects. Adding to winning positions as price validates your research improves the potential for profit. However, scaling necessitates rigorous guidelines to avoid overexposure. Each subsequent entry must meet the same requirements as the original position.

I scale into positions when price activity supports my analysis. A robust advance from a support zone may justify adding at the next higher low. The idea is to maintain a realistic total exposure while maximising profitable opportunities.

Position management grows more complicated with time. You will learn how to read market trends and change your exits accordingly. Some trades demand rapid rewards, while others require more time to develop. Success comes from aligning your management style with current market behaviour.

The concepts presented here serve as a basis for properly executing trades. Each entry and exit choice should align with your overall trading strategy while responding to particular market conditions. The next chapter delves into risk management strategies for protecting your wealth while pursuing profitable opportunities.

You'll develop a strong trading strategy by applying these entry and exit tactics consistently, as well as good risk management. Instead of chasing ideal entries or exits, focus on executing your goal. Market success is achieved by the diligent implementation of established strategies across several trades.

Chapter 8

Risk Management for Zone Trading

Position Sizing Based On Zones

Risk management is the cornerstone of effective forex trading. Through my trading experience, I've learnt that adequate position sizing is more important than flawless entry positions. Your position size should take into account both the strength of the zone and the distance to your stop loss. Stronger zones frequently justify larger positions, whereas weaker zones require more conservative sizing.

When trading within zones, adjust your position size to reflect market volatility. Higher volatility necessitates smaller positions to maintain consistent risk levels. My technique connects position size to the zone's features, including width, historical significance, and present market conditions.

Setting Stops with Zone Analysis.

Stop placement necessitates balancing protection with tolerance for regular price volatility. Placing stops too close together within a zone frequently results in premature exits. You'll have better luck establishing stops outside of the zone's limits, where price action genuinely invalidates your analysis.

I've observed that successful stop placement requires an awareness of how prices normally behave inside various zones.

Some zones see abrupt reversals, while others face more extended testing. Your stops must account for these trends while remaining within acceptable risk levels.

Risk-reward calculations

Each trade must provide a substantial payoff potential relative to risk. Strong zones provide as unambiguous reference points for determining risk-reward ratios. Your aim should be at least the next substantial zone, indicating a worthwhile profit potential for the risk taken.

The most profitable setups are generally formed when several things come together, such as strong support or resistance, obvious mood cues, and attractive price activity. These situations usually provide higher risk-reward ratios, which can surpass 3:1 or even 4:1.

Managing Drawdowns

Drawdowns test every trader's willpower. You will be able to weather these periods while saving wealth for future opportunities if you practise appropriate risk management. My strategy reduces risk during drawdowns by reducing position sizes and improving trade entry conditions.

Your trading strategy must include maximum drawdown levels that trigger defensive actions. These could include lowering position sizes, trading fewer setups, or temporarily suspending trading. Capital protection is prioritised amid difficult market conditions.

Portfolio Heat Management

Managing total portfolio exposure is critical for long-term survival. Monitor your overall risk across all holdings to ensure that no single trade or series of trades can cause significant damage to your account. I establish rigorous restrictions on total exposure, often risking no more than

2-3% of my portfolio on any given setup

Portfolio heat rises as currency pairs become more correlated. Trading many pairs in the same direction increases both possible profits and hazards. When calculating overall exposure, your analysis must take these linkages into account.

The techniques presented here provide critical risk management tools for zone trading. Success requires the persistent implementation of these principles in all market conditions. The following chapter delves into advanced zone concepts, which build on the foundation of solid risk management.

Trading without effective risk management ensures eventual failure. Undefined risk leads to account annihilation, regardless of how strong your analysis or how exact your entries are. Concentrate on maintaining capital through rigorous risk management, allowing your advantage to build over time.

These risk management techniques keep your trading cash safe while pursuing profitable possibilities. Together with strong zone analysis and exact execution, they form a solid foundation for persistent trading success. Prioritise risk management before pursuing ideal trade setups.

Chapter 9

Advanced Zone Concepts

Order Flow Analysis

Order flow exposes the underlying dynamics of price fluctuation within zones. Years of observation have taught me to recognise the imprints of huge institutional traders. These players leave distinct patterns, such as absorption of heavy sell orders at support or accumulation before to huge swings. Understanding order flow enhances your zone analysis.

Price movements alter when significant orders join the market. Sharp spikes frequently suggest institutional activity, whereas slow movements usually reflect retail trading. You'll note that certain zones receive more institutional attention, particularly around big technical levels or during significant economic events.

Market Structure Analysis.

The market structure gives context for zone trading. Higher period trends influence how prices behave in lower timeframe zones. My analysis always begins with determining the prevailing market structure (trending, range, or transitional). This framework sets expectations for price behaviour in specific zones.

Strong trends provide dynamic support and resistance zones. Previous resistance frequently becomes support, while previous support converts into resistance.

These structural adjustments open up opportunities for traders who comprehend market evolution.

Institutional Trade Zones

Institutional traders target distinct price zones for their activities. Round numbers, daily opening prices, and weekly pivots generate a lot of order activity. Through my expertise, I've noticed patterns in how institutions amass and disperse positions within these zones.

When aligned with institutional action, your trading improves. Larger players require time and space to establish or exit positions. Their activity produces discernible patterns: absorption at support, distribution at resistance. These patterns provide insights on probable market direction.

Complex Zone Patterns

More in-depth market analysis reveals advanced zone patterns. Triple tests of support or resistance are frequently used before significant moves. Failed breakouts of key zones can result in dramatic reversals. Understanding these complicated patterns improves your capacity to predict market behaviour.

I pay close attention to how prices behave after breaking big zones. Strong movements frequently follow false breakouts, trapping traders on the wrong side. These situations offer good risk-reward opportunities to prepared traders.

Harmonics and zones.

Harmonic patterns offer further validation for zone trading. These geometric patterns frequently end near substantial support or resistance zones.

While harmonics are not primary indicators, when aligned with strong zones and obvious market structure, they can improve your analysis.

The most powerful setups occur when a number of technical aspects align. A harmonic pattern that ends at strong support, as proven by positive divergence and obvious price action, presents enticing trade opportunities. Your analysis should incorporate these numerous components while remaining focused on the fundamental zone ideas.

Advanced zone analysis can help you gain a better grasp of the market. Each notion builds on the core zone trading principles while adding sophistication to your strategy. Success comes from gradually integrating these advanced concepts, ensuring a firm understanding of the fundamentals before adding complexity.

Understanding these advanced principles is essential for professional trading. However, applications should be chosen and disciplined. Not every pattern or indicator merits equal weight. Concentrate on situations in which numerous factors align, resulting in high-probability opportunities.

The following chapter delves into practical execution using precise trading plans and systematic approach development. These advanced concepts work as tools in your trading arsenal, supplementing rather than replacing key zone trading principles.

Chapter 10

Building Your Trading Plan

Create Your Zone Trading Strategy

A strong trading plan turns theory into actual success. I've learnt through years of trading that a methodical approach is superior to an emotional one. Your plan must include explicit criteria for trade identification, entry triggers, position sizing, and exit strategies. Begin by identifying your ideal price zones, which include support, resistance, and dynamic areas.

The greatest trading strategy adapt to changing market conditions.

Based on evident market structure, my approach alternates between trending and ranging strategies. You'll need certain rules for determining market context and tailoring your strategies accordingly. Each piece of your plan should include specific actions rather than broad instructions.

Test Your Zone System

Before putting real money at risk, system testing confirms your trading approach. Track each trade setup that satisfies your criteria, including entrances, exits, and market conditions. During my testing phase, I uncovered weaknesses in my initial assumptions and adjusted my approach based on the actual outcomes.

Paper trading helps to build confidence in your system. Follow your rules precisely, conducting each trade as if real money was at stake. Document what works and what needs to be changed.

To ensure consistent performance, your testing should cover a wide range of market conditions.

Recordkeeping and Trade Analysis

Detailed trade records reveal opportunities for improvement. Each trade entry should include the zone strength, market mood, and price action signs that influenced your decision. I keep detailed records of both successful and failing trades, analysing patterns that result in better outcomes.

A regular examination of your trading performance exposes both strengths and faults. Analyse your best trades to figure out what made them effective.

Examine your losses to find preventable errors. Your records become an invaluable tool for continuous improvement.

Continuous Improvement Process

Trading mastery necessitates continuous refinement. Markets develop, resulting in new difficulties and possibilities. My approach includes regular review periods during which I assess performance and alter strategies as appropriate. Maintain an open mind about improvement while remaining consistent with your basic approach.

In the world of trading, professional growth never ends. Study successful traders, study market analyses, and broaden your expertise. Your development approach should strike a balance between learning new concepts and honing existing skills. Concentrate on gradual growth rather than abrupt adjustments.

Psychology & Discipline

Trading psychology frequently influences success and failure. Strong analysis is meaningless without rigorous implementation. I've learnt through experience that emotional control is more important than technical expertise. Your plan must include clear rules for achieving psychological balance.

Discipline entails sticking to your rules even when emotions force you to do otherwise. Set defined risk management parameters and stick to them, regardless of market conditions. Your success is dependent on the regular implementation of proven strategies rather than rash ones.

The topics discussed here give a framework for a professional trading approach. Each part builds on prior chapters while emphasising practical application.

The following chapter delves into real-world trading examples that illustrate these principles in action.

Trading success stems from the consistent application of sound concepts. Build your plan carefully, test it extensively, and keep rigorous discipline in implementation. Focus on process rather than outcomes, recognising that regular use of right methods leads to long-term success.

Keep in mind that a trading plan evolves over time. Maintain the flexibility necessary to absorb new discoveries while adhering to the underlying principles that drive success. Your forex trading adventure will involve patience and persistence, as well as a well-structured plan.

Chapter 11

Real-World Trading Scenarios.

Case Study on Major Currency Pairs

Major pairs have distinct personalities in their zone reactions. The most traded pair, EUR/USD, frequently follows technical zones with amazing precision. Throughout several trading sessions, I've noticed how this pair establishes definite support and resistance zones, especially around major psychological levels.

Understanding the various qualities of majors is required while trading them. USD/JPY reacts substantially to interest rate differentials and risk sentiment.

Your analysis must include these fundamental aspects while focussing on technical zone patterns. The most powerful setups arise when fundamental and technical aspects align.

Case Study: Cross Rates.

Cross rates provide unique trading opportunities. The EUR/GBP swings reflect the relative economic strength of Europe and Britain. These pairs frequently exhibit strong trending moves, resulting in several zone-based trading opportunities. My experience indicates that crosses frequently respect technical levels more clearly than major pairs.

You'll observe that crosses occasionally lead major pairs in significant moves. Examine how EUR/GBP behaves before major EUR/USD movements. These correlations offer useful information for timing trades. Cross-rate analysis enhances your overall market understanding.

Case Study: Exotic Pairs.

Exotic pairs necessitate close attention to zone analysis. Their greater spreads and reduced liquidity result in unusual trading conditions. I've learnt from trading USD/ZAR that exotic pairs frequently establish broader zones due to more volatility. Your position sizing must change accordingly.

These pairs exhibit stronger responses to local economic conditions. USD/SGD swings are closely related to Asian economic conditions. To succeed in exotic pairs, zone analysis must be combined with a greater understanding of the fundamentals. Pay close attention to area economic changes.

Market Condition Analysis

Various market conditions necessitate different trading strategies. Trending markets generate dynamic support and resistance zones. Ranging market segments create distinct trades limits. My technique responds to these conditions while adhering to the key zone trading ideas. Before implementing specific methods, you must conduct an analysis to determine the current market state.

Market shifts frequently present compelling trading opportunities. When ranges break into trends, powerful directional moves are usually followed. Look for zone breaks that indicate these changes. The greatest profitable trades are often made by correctly identifying market condition changes.

Trading Journal

Real trading journals demonstrate the practical implementation of zone ideas. My entries include particular elements that influenced judgements, such as zone strength, emotion indicators, and price action signals. Your diary should include both technical analysis and psychological aspects that influence trades.

Sample journal entry: "EUR/USD long at 1.0850." Strong support zone (several daily touches). Positive divergence on the RSI. With above-average volume, I entered the pin bar reversal trade. The initial stop below the zone is at 1.0820. First, target previous resistance at 1.0900."

Detailed journaling helps to identify patterns in successful trades. Monitor your mental state, market conditions, and unique triggers for each trade.

This documentation provides essential reference material for optimising your trading strategy.

The situations presented here demonstrate the practical implementation of zone trading ideas. Each case necessitates tailoring broad concepts to unique market conditions. Recognising these trends and using effective methods leads to success.

Professional trading requires ongoing market analysis and adaptation. Stay focused on identifying high-probability setups while adhering to stringent risk management. The final chapter discusses frequent issues and solutions in zone trading implementation.

Chapter 12

Common Challenges and Solutions.

Dealing With False Breakouts

False breakouts challenge every trader's discipline. I've learnt from years of market watching that zones frequently repel price several times before genuine breakouts occur. While protecting money, your approach must account for these fake-outs. Smart traders wait for confirmation before pursuing breakouts.

The most severe false breaks usually occur at major technical levels. Price exceeds support or resistance, triggers stops, and then reverses abruptly.

My method includes keeping an eye out for these traps and occasionally leveraging them as counter-trend opportunities. Patience throughout breakout attempts results in improved trade selection.

Managing News Events

News events present particular obstacles for zone trading. Major announcements can temporarily disable technical levels. Through my experience, I've established specialised rules for trading around news. Your plan must include specific criteria for position sizing and risk management during high-impact events.

Economic releases frequently induce price spikes across zones before returning to former levels. Be cautious during major news events, especially if you are in close proximity to important zones.

To trade with higher volatility in these scenarios, larger stops and smaller position sizes are necessary.

Handling volatile markets.

Market volatility necessitates a flexible trading approach. Strong price swings create larger zones and necessitate different position sizing. My method adjusts to volatility levels while adhering to key trading concepts. Your success is dependent on recognising when markets enter higher volatility stages.

Volatile conditions frequently provide fantastic trading opportunities for experienced traders. Wider price fluctuations indicate greater potential rewards, but also increased risk. During these times, focus on the strongest zones rather than marginal setups that may work in calmer markets.

Overcoming Emotional Trading.

Emotions test every trader's decision-making abilities. Fear produces missed opportunities, whereas greed leads to excessive trading. I've learnt through years of trading that rigorous adherence to established guidelines helps manage emotional responses. Your trading strategy must include clear instructions for preserving emotional discipline.

Trading psychology affects all aspects of market analysis and execution. When emotions take precedence over logic, even the most robust technical arrangements fail. Avoid chasing emotional urges and instead focus on following your system. Consistently using established tactics leads to success.

Building Consistency

Professional traders distinguish themselves from novices by maintaining consistency. Each trades must adhere to your defined rules and procedures. My approach prioritises systematic analysis and execution over individual trade results. Your focus should be on the process rather than the outcome.

Daily routine improves trading consistency. Begin each session with a comprehensive market study. Review active zones, consult the economic calendar, and assess market conditions. This systematic approach promotes improved decision-making and more consistent outcomes.

The issues discussed here affect all traders at different periods. Success comes not from avoiding these challenges, but from dealing with them successfully.

Each challenge provides opportunities for you to enhance your trading strategy and approach.

Professional trading necessitates overcoming these common challenges while remaining focused on basic techniques. Stay committed to your trading strategy, respond to changing market conditions, and exercise strong execution discipline. These ideas provide the foundation for long-term trading success.

Remember that every trader's journey has hurdles. Learn from each event, adjust your approach as needed, and remain confident in your tried-and-true trading strategies. Patience, discipline, and constant improvement are required for achieving sustained profitability.

Conclusion

Your Journey to Mastery

The path to mastering zone trading in forex goes well beyond basic technical analysis. We've explored the complex dance of support and resistance, market sentiment, and price action across the book's chapters. Now that you've reached this threshold of understanding, take a moment to consider how these pieces fit together in the tapestry of successful trading.

My journey from struggling trader to consistent professional showed me that true mastery comes from combining many areas of market analysis. The zones we've covered are more than just lines on a chart; they reflect locations where key market participants make critical decisions. You obtain insight into the market's psyche by understanding these zones.

Trading success is built around three key pillars. First, the capacity to detect and analyse key price zones where market forces converge. Second, analyse market sentiment to understand the collective psychology that drives price movement. Third, interpret price action cues to make specific trading judgements. These variables work together to produce significant trading opportunities.

The currency market is always evolving, creating new challenges and possibilities. While adhering to key ideas, your trading approach must be flexible. Some days will test your patience, while others will reward your perseverance. Throughout, keep the methods and strategies we've covered in mind and use them consistently.

Risk management serves as the protector of your trading capital. Long-term success remains elusive without adequate risk management, regardless of how excellent your analysis or exact your inputs are. Always remember that capital preservation takes precedence over profit maximisation. Small, consistent profits accumulate over time, however huge losses might wipe out your trading account.

Market mastery necessitates ongoing learning and change. Every trading session provides new insights on market behaviour. Your success as a trader is dependent on staying open to these teachings while keeping disciplined in your primary approach. Document your trades, analyse your performance, and fine-tune your strategies based on actual market experience.

The topics given in this book provide a foundation for professional trading. However, knowledge alone does not ensure success. Your journey entails converting this understanding into practical trading skills through rigorous application and ongoing development. Stay patient throughout this process, recognising that mastery comes from consistent work over time.

Trading psychology is critical to your development. Fear, greed, and other emotions can impair your decision-making skills. To combat these effects, strictly adhere to your trading plan. Instead of acting on emotional impulses, let your analysis lead your actions. Maintaining emotional stability in the face of changing market conditions is critical to success.

Remember that every successful trader encountered comparable challenges on their path to success. The difference is not in avoiding obstacles, but in handling them efficiently. Use the strategies and approaches we've covered to overcome market challenges while honing your trading skills. Every hurdle overcome enhances your trading base.

Your trading journey extends beyond these pages. The markets will give you with new opportunities to put your skills to the test and challenge your preconceptions. Approach each trading day with a fresh viewpoint while remaining confident in your tried-and-true strategies. True mastery arises from integrating knowledge and practical experience.

The path ahead is fraught with both challenges and possibilities. Maintain your dedication to your trader development. Apply these concepts rigorously, handle risk prudently, and remain disciplined in your approach.

Success in forex trading is reserved for those who persevere in the face of adversity while constantly polishing their skills.

May your trading journey bring you both success and personal growth. Armed with the knowledge and strategies we've explored together, the markets welcome your participation. Trade wisely, maintain discipline, and never stop learning from the greatest teacher of all: the market itself.

Video Access Page

Thank you for purchasing my book! As a token of my appreciation, I've made available exclusive video content just for you.

To access your complimentary videos, simply visit:

https://mega.nz/folder/IYZRQZTL#UIoA3WK6Gb_OfS2Xxq-iRA

Thank you for your support, and I hope these additional resources enhance your reading experience!

Best regards,

James willy

www.ingramcontent.com/pod-product-compliance
Lightning Source LLC
Chambersburg PA
CBHW071055240526
45469CB00006BD/2311